UFOs

UFOs

BY SUSAN HARRIS
ILLUSTRATED BY SALLY LAW

AN EASY-READ FACT BOOK

FRANKLIN WATTS
NEW YORK / LONDON / TORONTO / SYDNEY / 1980

Thanks are due to the following for kind permission
to reproduce photographs:

Fortean Picture Library; Keystone Press Agency; Popperfoto

Library of Congress Cataloging in Publication Data
Harris, Susan.
UFOs.
(An Easy-read Fact Book).
Includes index
SUMMARY: Presents easy-to-read accounts of sightings
of and close encounters with unidentified flying objects
and alien creatures.
1. Unidentified flying objects—Juvenile literature.
[1. Unidentified flying objects]   I. Law, Sally.
II. Title.
TL789.H37   001.9'42   79-17428
ISBN 0-531-04098-4

R.L.2.9 Spache Revised Formula

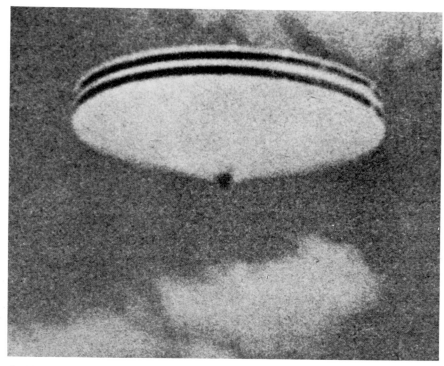

**An Unidentified Flying Object (UFO)
photographed over Oregon, in 1964.**

There is a very exciting mystery in our world. The mystery concerns strange objects seen in the sky. Many people claim to have seen these unexplained objects. For hundreds of years people have made such reports. What did they really see?

(5)

One of the most famous **sightings** happened in 1947. Kenneth Arnold was flying his small plane over Washington State. Suddenly he spotted a strange sight.

He saw nine silver discs flying together in the sky. They were moving up and down. "Like a saucer skipping over water," he said. The unusual discs had wings, but no tails. They reflected the sun like mirrors. They did not bother him and soon disappeared.

Arnold landed his plane and told reporters what he had seen. Newspapers printed the story. They called the objects **flying saucers.** Then an interesting thing happened.

Other people all over the country had stories to tell, too. Many of them had been seeing strange objects in the sky. These sightings had occurred long before Arnold's. The newspapers printed hundreds of these stories. Since 1947, there have been more than 10,000 reports of sightings.

(7)

Not all of the strange objects looked like saucers. They were reported in various shapes and sizes.

A new term—**UFO**—was used to describe these objects. UFO is short for an **Unidentified Flying Object.** An object in the sky that cannot be explained is usually called a UFO. Over the years, there have been many arguments. Are UFOs real or imagined?

By 1977, 56 percent of the people in the United States said they believed in UFOs. Eleven percent said they had *seen* a UFO. That is about 15 million people! Are persons who see and report UFOs strange? The answer seems to be no.

Sightings have been reported by people in the Army, Navy, Marines, and Air Force. Scientists, engineers, and airline pilots have reported UFO sightings. And, of course, ordinary citizens have seen UFOs.

All of these people make reports because they have seen something. They are worried, or curious, about what they have seen.

(9)

In 1966 there were a very large number of reported sightings. One involved 87 students at a Michigan college. They all claimed to have seen a glowing, football-shaped object. It **hovered** (floated) in the sky over a nearby swamp. Then it flew directly at one of the college buildings. Suddenly it stopped and flew back over the swamp. It would brighten then dim its lights. The students watched the object for four hours.

Another 1966 sighting took place one morning in April. Two Ohio policemen were resting in their parked car. Suddenly a UFO glided out of the nearby woods. It came toward the car. As the UFO got nearer, it became brighter and brighter. Then it was right over the car. It made a strange humming noise. And it was as big as a house.

Finally the UFO began to move away. The policemen followed it in their car. They chased it for 40 miles (64 km) at speeds of up to 100 miles (161 km) per hour. Then suddenly the huge bright shape went straight up into the sky and disappeared.

The subject of UFOs was argued everywhere in the country in 1966. All the magazines and newspapers carried stories. Radio and TV shows were full of UFO talk. The subject became known as **The UFO Controversy** (KON-tro-vur-cee).

(10)

(11)

UFOs were seen not only in the United States. There were sightings reported all over the world.

Captain Denis Wood was a British pilot. He had flown for twenty years. One day in July 1976, Captain Wood was flying over Portugal. He looked out of the window and saw something in the sky. It was a round, brilliant white object. It came between the plane and the sun. Captain Wood decided that it was not a **satellite** (spacecraft). Nor was it a balloon or a falling star.

The crew in the plane also saw the bright light. Suddenly they all saw two cigar-shaped objects. The objects seemed to come out of nothing. They were big and solid and gave off their own light. After about eight minutes, the objects took off at a very high speed and disappeared.

This sighting was also reported by two other pilots flying in the same area that day.

**A series of pictures of a
UFO flying over Lisbon,
Portugal, in November 1978.**

(12)

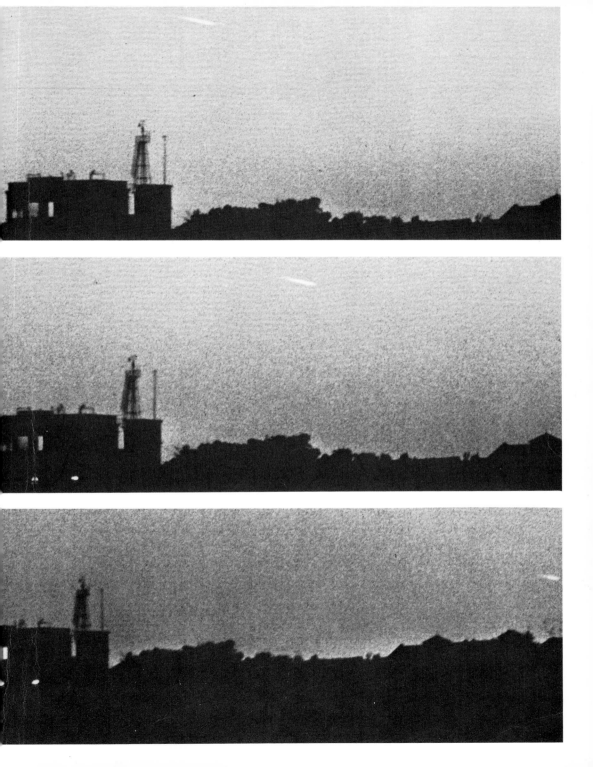

The people who made these reports were respected citizens. They were not imagining, and they certainly did see something. But the question is, what did they see?

People have seen many different things. UFOs seem to come in various shapes and sizes. Some are just a few feet wide. Others are nearly 200 feet (60 m) wide!

Sometimes UFOs fly alone. Sometimes many are seen flying together in formation. Often they look blurry and shapeless.

Others look like saucers, planets, rockets, or stars. Are the small UFOs **scout ships** (observers)? Are the large UFOs **mother ships?** That is what some people think. But others disagree.

(15)

Many people have reported seeing creatures inside or near a UFO that has landed. These creatures usually have shapes similar to humans. They have two arms, two legs, and a head. But everybody agrees they don't really look human. These creatures are called **ufonauts** (U-foe-nauts).

Ufonauts seem to come in many different forms. Some are dressed in silver suits and glow. Others have strange things sticking out of their heads. And some look like very small human beings.

Many people think ufonauts are very intelligent. If they do exist, it has not yet been proven.

People who are very interested in UFOs are sometimes called **ufologists** (U-FOL-o-jists). Ufologists carefully study each reported sighting. They are especially interested in a **Close Encounter** (CE).

A CE means that the UFO has been seen from a short distance away—about 300 to 500 feet (90 to 150 m). There are three kinds of close encounters: **CE1, CE2,** and **CE3.**

A **close encounter of the first kind** (CE1) is the sighting of a UFO with a definite shape. It is not just a glow or a shadow. CE1s can be picked up on a **radar screen** (aircraft detector). They can also be seen in person.

An example of a CE1 happened in January 1971. Some sailors saw a UFO flying over Trinidad, an island in the South Atlantic Ocean.

(19)

(20)

The UFO the sailors saw was shaped like the planet Saturn. It had a ring around it. It was dark, and surrounded by a green mist. The sailors guessed that it was moving at 600 to 700 miles (960 to 1,130 km) per hour. It was about 120 feet (36 m) across and 24 feet (7 m) high.

One of the men had a camera. He quickly snapped pictures of the UFO. Four came out very clear. They are some of the best pictures ever taken of a UFO. Experts who have examined these photographs say they are not fakes (made up).

A **close encounter of the second kind** (CE2) means there is a sign left behind after the UFO has gone. The sign might be a mark on the ground. Plants may be flattened or burned. Sometimes lights or television sets won't work. There might even be burns on the face or hands of a witness.

CE2s sometimes make animals behave very strangely.

A picture of the sighting over Trinidad

(21)

One January evening in 1977, a British couple were walking their dog, Sam. On their return home, Sam howled and ran off. The couple turned to call the dog back. Then they saw what had upset him.

About 300 feet (91 m) away was a huge saucer-shaped object. It was about 50 feet (15 m) across. It hovered about 80 feet (24 m) above the ground and was completely silent. There were no windows, no doors, no lights, and no landing wheels.

It stayed still for about 20 minutes. Then it rose into the air and suddenly disappeared.

The frightened couple ran into their house. Their son complained about the television set. For almost half an hour, he had not gotten any picture.

Sam was gone for two days. When he came home, he was still upset. He was afraid to go into the field where the UFO had been. He refused to go out at all at night.

There are two Air Force bases nearby. No one at the bases had noticed anything unusual.

What did the couple see? What frightened the dog? It all remains a mystery.

A close encounter of the third kind (CE3) is the most exciting. It can also be the most frightening. A CE3 is the sighting of creatures (ufonauts) in or near the UFO.

One November evening in 1976, a couple were driving along a quiet country road in England. Suddenly the car began to shake. Then the headlights became very bright. An invisible force made the car go off the road into a ditch. As the car stopped, the couple looked up and saw a strange sight.

A glowing, cigar-shaped object was hovering above the road. Three creatures stared down at them from a window in the UFO. Suddenly, one of them appeared by the side of the car.

It was about 6 feet (2 m) tall, thin, with long fair hair, and a dark beard. It wore a silver suit fastened with a long zipper. It looked quickly into the car at them. Then it and the UFO disappeared.

This is a very unusual sighting. Yet that same evening, there had been eight other UFO sightings near there. Seven people had seen a glowing, cigar-shaped UFO. One reported seeing a strange-looking man in a silver suit!

(25)

Sometimes ufonauts appear to want to make contact with people. But most of the time they seem to like just watching. Some people feel there are other intelligent beings in the universe. They are the people who believe in CE3s.

A woman tells of an odd CE3 experience. While hanging up her wash in the garden, she saw a shining blue light. It was moving rapidly toward her.

"There I was, completely covered in blue light," she said. "I saw three beings who looked like men. They did not speak. They were about 5 feet (1.5 m) tall and wore blue clothes. They grasped me by the arms and we were lifted up into a kind of room. More of the men were in the room. I was given the feeling, I don't know how, that I would come to no harm. A little later, I found myself back in my garden. I felt a sharp blow on the back of my neck. I was stunned but not hurt. When I looked around, the thing set off at great speed and disappeared."

That is her story. No one can prove it. But then, no one can disprove it, either!

(27)

What can these sightings be? Is our earth really being visited by creatures from other worlds? Those who say no have good arguments on their side.

Many things can cause people to *think* they are seeing UFOs. Often they are looking at **astronomical** (ASS-trow-nom-e-kal) objects. Bright stars, planets, comets, fireballs, and meteors (falling stars) might look like UFOs. A flash of the Arctic Lights might look like a strange craft. People often think they are seeing UFOs when they are seeing planets during unusual weather.

But we are still left with a puzzle. Can you explain the pictures on the facing page?

Two photographs of unidentified flying objects. Above, right: over New Mexico in 1957. Below, right: England, 1954.

The planet Venus might look like a UFO. It is very bright and sometimes gives out a shining red or blue light.

Satellites are often thought to be UFOs. There are many artificial satellites going around the earth.

Satellites should be easy to spot. Special tracking stations always keep a watch on where they are and where they are going. However, it is true that satellites have been mistaken for UFO sightings.

Our new space age has filled the skies with many strange and wonderful objects. Many of these objects might look like a UFO.

(31)

Airplanes are the cause of many UFO sightings. Their lights can look very strange during foggy or rainy weather. When the sun shines on the metal surface, it may bounce off with a very bright light.

A jet plane leaves a trail of water vapor. This sometimes becomes strangely bright when light hits it. But airplanes are easily spotted by where they are. Their travel is usually watched on radar screens.

Balloons are often mistaken for UFOs. Airfields and weather stations send up special balloons every day. These large balloons are used to study the weather. They are not always easy to identify.

(33)

Ball lightning may explain many UFO sightings. Like flashes of lightning, it is an electrical discharge. Ball lightning looks like a slowly moving bright ball.

Sometimes it blows up in the air. This may be why some people have seen UFOs that suddenly disappear. Sometimes ball lightning burns objects it comes near.

Ball lightning produces many of the effects that are reported with UFO sightings. It leaves a smell. It causes electrical interference. It leaves burn marks on the ground.

Many mysterious sightings may be flashes of ball lightning. However, it has been difficult to prove this.

Ball lightning can be mistaken for a UFO.

(35)

(36)

There are other possible explanations for UFO sightings. Flocks of flying birds can look like something else. Clouds sometimes look very strange, especially when hit by sunlight. Electric trains often give off bright flashes of light. Even a kite flying in the sky might look like something else.

Sometimes a person sees an object in the distance. But this object is not really there. This is called a **mirage** (MEH-raj). It is caused by light reflected on layers of air.

There are many organizations especially interested in reports of UFOs. These organizations study the reports and try to find explanations.

On page 38 is a list of sightings reported in the United States during August 1977. Of the 76 sightings, 62 could be easily explained. For six, there was not enough information. Eight cases were thought to be UFOs.

(37)

Sightings reported in the United States during August 1977

Causes	Number of reports
Stars	19
Advertising planes	13
Meteors	8
Aircraft	7
Flares	4
Balloons	3
Kites	1
Mirages	1
Missiles	1
Floodlights	1
Helicopters	1
Prank balloons	1
Aircraft vaporization	1
Birds	1
Not enough information supplied	6
UFOs	8
Total	76

(38)

(39)

Some UFO reports are not believed by most people. One such story is that of a California man, George Adamski.

One day in 1952 he was driving in the desert with friends. About 1 mile (1·6 km) ahead, they saw a UFO land. Leaving his friends behind, Adamski rushed to the landing spot.

George Adamski's photo of a UFO. Many experts did not believe his story. But no one could prove that it was not true.

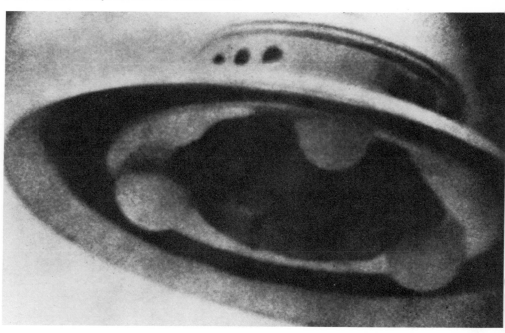

(40)

When Adamski neared the craft, a small, handsome man appeared. He talked "silently" to him.

Adamski got one blurry picture of the UFO. He also made a plaster cast of the ufonaut's footprint.

Some scientists said that Adamski's story was a **hoax** (trick). But no one has ever proven that.

Some people said that Adamski copied a bottle-cooler (shown below) for the shape of his UFO.

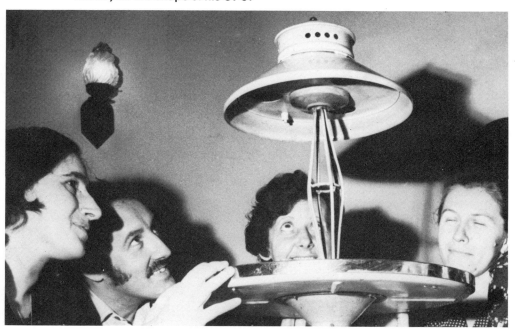

UFOs have been reported all over the world. But most governments do not think they exist. They are interested in only one thing. That is whether UFOs are dangerous. So far, no one seems to think so.

Yet, no one can prove that UFOs do not exist.

Model of a flying saucer built by the French

(42)

The Ufoport near Bordeaux, France

France is one of the few countries that takes UFOs seriously. The French government has a National Space Studies Unit. The French have actually built a **ufoport.** It is a special place for a UFO to land. It is open 24 hours a day.

The French believe that UFOs have never made contact for a reason. There was no proper place for them to land.

Now they have a place. But still, nothing has happened!

(43)

We may never know for sure if UFOs really exist. Most sightings have been made by responsible citizens. But there are too many questions that cannot be answered.

There are many opinions about what UFOs are and why they have come. But there is little or no scientific proof to support these opinions.

What, then, can we believe? It is hard to believe most of the stories. This is especially true of ufonaut contacts. It is also hard to believe that all UFOs are just human-made or natural objects.

In October 1973, a television reporter said: "Many people would like the UFOs to go away. But the UFOs won't go away, and many scientists are taking them very seriously. It's likely that we will hear more and more about UFOs."

Whatever we hear, each of us will have our own thoughts on the subject. The exciting mystery continues!

(44)

(45)

Rules to Follow Just in Case . . .

1. If you see a UFO land, do not go near it. Keep under cover, if possible.
2. Try to find another person to look with you. Another witness makes your story more believable.
3. Do not interfere with the UFO's activities. If ufonauts try to contact you, don't panic.
4. Try to remember as many details as possible. Notice the size and shape of the UFO. Note clothing and appearance of ufonauts.
5. Check time when seen and for how long. Also, how long it took to disappear.
6. Try to take a picture if you have a camera with you.
7. Remember the spot of the landing, if possible.
8. Write down all you can remember about the sighting. Do it right away. Drawings are also helpful.
9. Tell your parents or the police about your experience.

(46)

(47)

INDEX

Adamski, George, 40–41
Air Force, 8
Aircraft, 32, 38
Animal Behavior, 21–23, 37
Army, 8
Arnold, Kenneth, 6

Ball lightning, 34
Balloons, 4, 32, 38

CE. *See* Close encounters
Close encounters, 18–26
Comets, 28

Fireballs, 28
Flying saucers, 6, 14

Marines, 8
Meteors, 28, 38
Mirages, 37, 38

National Space Studies Unit, 43

Navy, 8
Northern lights, 28

Physics, 34
Planets, 14, 28
   Saturn, 21
   Sun, 12, 32
   Venus, 30

Radar, 18, 23, 32

Satellites, 12, 30
Sightings,
   England, 22–26
   France, 43
   guidelines for, 46
   Portugal, 12
   Trinidad, 18
   United States, 6, 8, 10, 37–38, 40
Southern lights, 28
Stars, 12, 14, 28, 38

Television, 10, 23

UFO. *See* Unidentified flying object
UFO controversy, 10
Ufologists, 18
Ufonauts, 16–17, 24–26, 41, 46
Ufoport, Bordeaux, France, 43
Unidentified flying object, 8, 38, 42, 44
   false reports, 40–41
   motion of, 6, 10, 12, 14, 21, 22, 26
   news reports, 6, 10, 44
   photographs, 12, 20, 21, 29, 40–41, 46
   signs of, 21

Weather, 28, 32, 34, 37
Wood, Denis, 12